To Billy & Barbers;
I hope you enjoy;
Revish Windham

I Wouldn't Take Nothing

for

My Journey

Poetry by

Revish Windham

ISBN: 0-75964-940-5

This book is printed on acid free paper.

To order this title:
www.1stbooks.com/bookview/7478
1-888-280-7715

1stBooks - rev. 8/17/01

Also by Revish Windham

Poetry

Shades of Black—1970
Shades of Anger—1972

To my wife, Janice, my sister, Huida, my daughter, Veronica, members of the Green-Wood and Whitten/Windham families, the Harlem Writers Guild for your early-on help, John O'Killen for allowing me to sit in during your class at Columbia University and for sharing with me your experience as a writer in your home, The Negro Book Club, Inc./Afro-American Book Club, Inc. for some invaluable support, special friends-Rev. James E.F. Lawrence, Julius and Doris Perry, Horace Mungin and Poets Corner for your belief in me, the creators of Black Forum Magazine, Gillian Grozier and the members of LINGUA, Stella Craft-Tremble for publishing my first poem in 1967, Diane Sands for reading my poem on the Alma John show, Johnny Samuels for first reading Ghetto Boy, a special thanks to Earl Smith and Michelle Cooper for your suggestions, Maxine Lawrence and Emily Amino for your faith, Elizabeth Rice for early guidance at North Sumpter High School and for being there for me even now, Alberto Cappas and A Place For Poets, Rita Spears, Roberto Colon and Jessyca Samuels-you each touched me in your own special way and to so many others I have been privileged to know during my journey. I am grateful that you shared parts of this great trip with me.

To my deceased parents—Lillie and Ike, Sr., and three brothers—Ike Jr., Willie James and Charles, I know I was blessed to have started out with you, virtue-blended. Though the time spent together was short, rest assured that since May 31, 1940 (my date of birth), I have taken the love you gave with me wherever I've traveled and will continue to do so until such time our hands re-touch, allowing our river-water to flow once more undisturbed.

CONTENTS

First there was the hill, then Panola, Dancy, Geiger, York, Montgomery, Cooksville, Carrolton, Macon, Aliceville, Reform, Tuscaloosa, Edgewater, Brimingham and a few in between

Chicago, Manhattan, Brooklyn, The Bronx, Augusta and short stops in between

Atlanta, Newark, Shreveport, Cincinnati, Miami Beach, Boston, Great Lakes, Bainbridge, Norfolk, Virginia Beach, Washington, D.C. and lots of others places

Pain oozed out as darkness enfolding daylight

Perpetuated love insures the taste of a first breath every morning

Spirituality, change, blues, leaving footsteps, forgiven, times in sadness, Joy when Black folks travel

I've come to understand the journey

First there was the hill.
Then came
Panola
Dancy
Cochran
Cooksville
York
Geiger
Aliceville
Carrolton
Macon
Tuscaloosa
Montgomery
Reform
Edgewater
Birmingham
and a few in between

Revish Windham

SATURDAY NIGHT

I remember watching
my father and the others
sit on weather-worn benches
in our part of Alabama, as if
they were watching sand moving
through an hourglass, reflecting
on a Saturday, without work;
gut reactions to or telling
others a horse/cow or some
pastoral jest or just talking about
how a boll weevil survives, exchanging
the past week's experience, drawing
new strength from friends.

The women sat, my mother included,
wearing Saturday-morning
starched dresses, polished shoes
preened faces and once-a-week
worn bracelets, sharing in stories
about womanhood and can't-wait gossip
forgetting for the moment
crops or how in no time
Saturday is gone, Sunday's
come and also gone—
another week's begun.

And us children, in and outside
playing games, laughing at images
our voices often piercing
imposing enough to hush the clouds;
then eating ice cream, chocolate cookies
and savoring ten cent sodas.
It didn't matter if the sun

moved into a shadow, causing
daylight to stretch its arms and
yawn about dusk coming...
night following.

For precious hours they all
floated with the breeze or
sought to hide from blazing sun—
their minds untouched by
evening star appearing;
they were celebrating an achievement
folded, soil turned, cotton picked
corn pulled, fences mended or
meals prepared in some
white folks' kitchens.

Then, especially late summer,
dew would begin its sprinkling,
laying thin veils over car roofs
causing thirsty grass to
shed day-time dryness,
taking away the sun.

Finally, all mindful
of night's nearness
Sunday morning church
starting soon, they'd get up
go inside Tom Hodges' Café
play blues on his juke box and dance,
enjoying what was left
                              of Saturday..

Farmers, their wives
their children, waiting
fulfilling until the moon rose
announcing time
to go home.

CHILDREN AND SUNDAY

Sunday in an Alabama town
finds them making ready
Black folks taking their best
from moth-balled closets
breakfast eaten, dinner set aside
families dressed for church, making
last minute adjustments to
frocks, pins in wide-brimmed hats
while children click new heels
against a front porch post
seeing if shoe heels
really are hurt resistant.

Sunday morning comes
early after last night,
children already thinking
about Sunday School, then hearing
a sermon, watching grown-ups
react, shout, saying amen
letting a week of pain come out
or some love come in, then
holding their hand-cupped sniggles,
learning, watching grown folks;
heads nodding, some
shouting
fainting

Sunday, a day for juvenile expression
enjoying, all dressed up; then
waiting til church time's over
coming home to dinner, playing
no thoughts about anything planned
just innate joy
before night and
sleeping into Monday.

SUMMER VACATION
(School's Out)

June, time to
play, fish, watch clouds
run under rain showers
splash in the puddles
it made, catch crayfish
watch grass smile when
its blades are touched
by the wind

Summertide, time to
catch June bugs
watch praying mantis stilt
across time's uneven sand
listen to crickets sing
watch "Lightin'Bugs" dance
a miniature New Years Eve
celebration

July brings magic nights,
owls chanting, frogs croaking
and from somewhere far
in between the sound of
children squealing, frolicking,
then the rumble of
an adult's baritone blend
about Old Man River
going to lay a burden down

In August, when night comes
there is a wait for tin-top roofs
to cool, a breeze to come along.
No one thinks about having
school come morning, vacation
is everyday, summer solstice.
Seems like children run forever
right through the nights
and back into day.

CHILD'S PLAY

We watched him
laughing so hard
not giving a hoot about anything
until he saw us coming;
we watched him bend in stitches
doing his best to control
a churning body, to keep
its pleasure-fullness from
going hog-wild…

                            he looked
the epitome of
a trying-to-be grownup
enjoying unripeness as that of
a six week old puppy.
How could he have known?
Even if he did, he would not want to
prepare himself for us.

So, we absorbed ourselves
in juvenile thoughtlessness
exercising without realizing or
caring how air travels lightly
through all of us, catching our
giggles, cackles, and sniggers
and everything else created
                 spontaneously
            even after sundown.
How can I forget,
           there were no restraints.

Finally, unable to resist,
we all, him included,
blindly cupped our hands
and performed in his
                    rain dance.

LISTENING TO GRANDMA
(Talk about her father's eyes)

My grandma sure was something else
I used to think she could see to
the other side of the world.
I think about the times
she'd sit me down beside her
unfolding wrinkling hands while
caressing her papa's picture frame
allowing her aging lips to relax
before starting to tell me
about him and some more
about what he had said.

I'd look at his posture, proud
a short brimmed hat slightly tilting
on his head, a thin mustache
stretching across his upper lip…
but it was something about his eyes
always caused me to stop, ask grandma
tell me again about his eyes?

She'd first look kind of sad
then start by saying he didn't
know what year he was born but
his mother was the child of a slave and
she cooked for the master, but
her papa, he never did know
who his father was
                then
            she'd be silent
            for moments...

During her silence
I'd sometimes wonder but
never did ask her
if her papa's childhood nights
were anything like mine
if children's laughter flowed
between darkness and light
if the sun and moon
played hide & seek and if
she was serious when she said
her own mama had said they did.
I wanted so much to ask
did your papa ever know
freedom like mine?

Grandma said the frame holding
his picture was handed down
and like her mama before her did
she keeps it balanced on her mantle piece
wire-propped against the wall.

She'd say, he first lit the light
I'm keeping the flame jumping
so you'll be able to see over into
the days he spoke about, not forget
the conditions, mental/physical pain
stench, living with death on
a ship full of Africans, brought
ashore, sold, the trepidation thereafter
rapes, deaths, clinging only
to tomorrow, praying to God
one day to find rest,
their souls, hoping...

Then, with her body wrapped
in senescence, self-satisfaction

would rise like an opening rose;
grandma'd tell me about his eyes
how they were strong as god-given fire
always accepting flames as they leapt
down through spiritual holes in the sky,
how he could clinch his hands
retch from the memory of slaves
hoping a storm's profusion would lift
slave masters into wispy clouds.
How his eyes could then pull, lifting the
morning sun, exposing arm-swaying oars
moving backward and forward
floating them back across
those dark waters
                towards Africa.

It was his dream, she'd half whisper
to taste that water he'd been told about
preserve the essence of his ancestors and
from this manna, mold together mortals
giving them back their souls, mores
culture, religion, language...
Yes child, she'd say to me,
                it was his dream.

Then one day, before she died
I finally understood why
she would, even when not
talking about her papa, like when
she was talking to friends,
she'd stop, look at me and smile
in complete exultation.
She'd say, she can see her papa's flame
still ignited, still glowing
for she could see it leaping down
through those same spiritual holes

out of God's hand-held sky
burning in her grandchild's eyes.

HER ROCKING CHAIR

It's a classic, a priceless gem,
that old rocking chair.
I remember Aunty Mamie
sitting in it, rocking slowly
in rhythm, moving back and forth
exposing over-wrought hands
expertly resting in her lap, pushing
those frail and weak legs, still strong enough
to move that rocker; and yes, Aunty Mamie's
a classic too, she's reminiscent of
eighty years, like a picture frame
unfolding, highlighting a dark
leather-brown face that's
so full of history.

She could smile and her expressions
spoke of many eventful years
when she was younger.
How she could sit there
in that rocking chair, thinking
in her quiet time, folding
remembering, when there were
open porches and out there
children played games, making
squealing noises in her back yard,
she would watch the young lovers
strolling down country roads
through the nurtured lanes…

Oh, she was always there
keeping rhythm in that old chair
filing her precious memories
on shelves to be read by those
she has influenced along the way.

She so often thought about
when she was up and about
she would make those visits to the city
when urban life meant
good times and prosperity, morning still
brought hope with its new dawn
contentment about a better today
was frequently on everybody's mind.

She thought of days when she didn't
have time to sit down, when she worked,
the pride she felt and how life had so much
meaning; but oh, how she would beam
when the subject of children came up,
she talked about having touched so
many of them. You could see in her face
how much she wanted those days
to again be, so she could do all over again
exactly what she did before for the children.
She just wanted to slow down time,
time that seemed so harsh, give it more
sensitivity to herself, an old aging woman.

Aunty Mamie taught children well,
even when she had gotten old,
had to sit down most of the time,
but she was still showing little Black girls
about expert cadence in a rocking chair,
infusing light without instruments
doing it all from memory; patiently

17

guiding their young minds into
where she had been, so they
may choose one day
to go there too.

Then there were those times
she would sit in that chair waiting
for the arrival of her friend, the postman,
for they knew each other's beginning.
They would talk about letters and
how they had watched 2-cent stamps fade
into yellow and how they could each
look into the others future and join hands
with self-contentedness.

Yes, my thinking about Aunty Mamie's
like looking at a classic car
remembering the treasured moments
keeping it waxed to be shown;
and that rocking chair...wow!

So, when you sit
in Aunty Mamie's chair
                              you think
while you're rocking back and forth
think about you too, folding with time
imparting to someone else
information about life and
that old rocking chair.

**Finally Chicago
Manhattan
Brooklyn
The Bronx
Augusta
and short stops in between**

Revish Windham

MOTHERS

are like endless summer
they take night, wrap it
tenderly in arms spanning
wide as eternity; they cup
sculptured hands that stroke
creating iconic-like prayer-painted
miracles, give the impossible
bring morning even when
the sun balks or night lingers
to laugh, stretching wholesale
always in maternal ardor
reaching over the edge
of the universe, forever
lifting the sun.

FREEDOM
(Change)

Within a moving school
is a fish with
no desire to be, and
so the day comes
he's different and free to
wonder, to swim away from
his school, wanting to return
but knowing that he
never will, even
if he does.

GOING NOWHERE FAST
(on arriving in New York City)

Blundering through walls
with no exit in view,
only a dimly scan of nothing
that's apparent to others.
I, without knowledge of day,
only the skimpy minute
that lasts for seconds…
voyaging to high lands,
vacationing,
views of Paris,
without constant living,
and not knowing
what the time affords.

IT'S CRY CLOWN, CRY

A face masked by colors,
a stained cloak given to
anyone who is asking for handouts
a clown cries underneath his laughter
a child never sees his tears and wonders
what clowns are made of.
The rest of the children skip about.
They chant a song
it's cry clown, cry.
They do not understand
and cannot realize for now, the hurt
beneath the funny / sad face
of the laughing clown.

DREAMS AND REALITY

1958, up-North stories were still
flourishing, passed-on by word of mouth
or in newspaper stories, sketches of
wide-opened visions of New York City
without color bars, where Negroes are
guaranteed equal opportunity, a chance
where bible created humans re-assure
a stranger's hand and anger is unheard of
when the sun fails to un-cloud the sky
or momentarily forget to hold back
rain so the sun can smile.

A Negro boy, shadow-quiet, waited in
cotton field patches, holding onto these
visions, and one day, clutching a shoe box,
holding food for his ride while fighting,
at early moments, the temptation to taste
enjoy the savorous richness of a mother's
deep fried chicken and whiting fish,
he took the back seat of a Greyhound bus.

His turn had finally come to endeavor
witness the crowding of highways
watch houses swarm into view, experience
modernization coming alive as only seen
in magazines, where urban living is described.
And feeling his insides churn, he held
tightly the images in that different world.

Then with eyes half-opened, awaking
from sleep into morning, he was amazed
seeing buildings appearing to cloud the
horizon, rising upward into the sky.

The bus too had inched between road-
held cars, leading over a bridge into
waiting streets that multiply themselves,
filled, grove-like, with people solo-waltzing
without touching each other or listening to
music the other had heard, yet each moving
as if a thousand spotlights were focused.

Space became sacred, he moved inside
of buildings, like tunneled hallways,
advancing without hearing laughter
or seeing smiles. The Negro boy could
only raise his arms in discovery, watch
doors close without answers, exposing
faces with eyes that failed to see his image.
Then his blindfold lifted, he headed for
a subway that rushes to limited places
offering blared colors of revulsion.

Reality blushed. For other people too,
of other races, other national origins, had
come with dreams, and experienced the pain
realizing a nation's enmity has long arms,
its deception lurks in the hearts of many,
never-thought-to-see evils secreting
fallacies of deceitfulness folding therein,
showing a paper-thin-air portrait of
a mirage lifting the infant Jesus.

1958, he smelled the rankness of evil
even in this picture-perfect up-North city
hate and fear thrives, shredded-hopes dance
without shame; a young man's fantasy
grown into dryness, he stood to watch
a beginning of his own revolution.

I learned about the Greek alphabet
in Atlanta, then on to
Newark
Shreveport
Cincinnati
Miami Beach
Great Lakes
Bainbridge
Norfolk
Virginia Beach
Washington, D.C.
and lots of other places

Revish Windham

THE REASON I MARCHED
(A tribute to Dr. Martin Luther King, Jr.)

I marched because I believed
in Martin Luther King's dream,
his unquestionable stance
that Negroes could no longer sit
only in the back of buses,
colored-only signs would have
to come down, respect must
be given to Negroes too,
freedom was no longer
a far off dream and could
become everybody's reality.

I marched because I could feel
entitlement for those years of labor
I had so often heard folks talk about,
penetrating and burning the innards
of my soul, leaving a smoking brand
flaming, exclaiming that I too
had the right to savor the blessing
of being an American, to laugh
about the joys it brings
regardless of my race or
the color of my skin.

I marched because I was reminded
of my mother, my father, all
the Negroes who had struggled
long before and after I was born,
African slaves and their descendants
all determined to maintain guts enough
to fight for freedom, dignity and
overdue justice; I wanted so much

to show my appreciation for the
sacrifices they made, hopes they left
so that I and all of those coming
after me would one day
have the chance they hadn't had
to experience Africa's freedom
here, to be afforded this so-called
American equal opportunity.

I marched because for first time
I could feel the chains releasing
sense a new beginning, the birth of
a new nation emerging, wrapped
in a Middle Passage strength blanket
of brother/sisterhood woven together
using thread Dr. King had preached
about, materials my parents had felt
and passed on its special warmth to me.

There was so much happening
I couldn't sit idle, had to get up
join hands, march down-town
sit-in at lunch counters, sing about
how "We Shall Overcome," stand up
to growling dogs, withstand the force
of water hoses, ignore red neck spit,
hate-gnawed curses, eyes that stabbed,
hatred thrown by those who
had never felt the touch of a God.

I had become etched in Dr. King's focus,
the time had come to reach without
falter for there might not be another
time and even if there were, I
might not have the nerve
when the next time came, to react

with the same force of inertia,
energized with the same vigor
preparing an impasse, making
a profound difference.

I marched for generations of people,
African slaves now dead, their
descendents still living and those
not yet born, to be photographed
marching for hope, freedom, respect,
integrity, appreciation, and more,
to join in, become a real part of
a Negro progression in history, feel
the uniqueness of me included
in the "I was there too" exclaims,
identified as a fighter, like my mother
and father were, proud, re-enforcing
a promise that the Negro will overcome;
that I may, in my time, witness
a "Marching Towards Justice"
cresting in frames, hanging on walls,
capturing the glory of a day when
the likes of a 14th Amendment is signed,
an event forever etched in the minds
of those living, preserved for the eyes
of those not yet born.

Do you now understand
                              why I marched?

Yes, I had
heard the hue and cry,
felt the pushing strength
behind the many uplifted arms,
assumed the assurance in the voices,
became united in the awakening precision

of prepared soldiers in the army…

It was for these reasons
                        that I marched.

DO YOU KNOW MY NAME
(A Real Story)

I walked into the opened door
Ocean Fronts' strip
in Norfolk, Virginia
smoke and a familiar coldness held
greed-like to my hand while
the tremble of a juke box
played a song
about a cheating heart.
An old man relaxed
his overlaid stomach and gabbed
about yesterday
trout fishing
baseball and
drinking too much watered down beer.

I watched the glasses
in front of everyone but mostly
eye-to-eye with mine.
I heard cars divide water outside
needing no one to create a parade.
The fat white man, sitting next to me
smelled like seaweed, he
shifted in his chair.
The bartender told humorless jokes
about the weather,
women laying sailors
in Virginia Beach while I
watched the beer sink
in silent traces down
long stem glasses.

Rain mist continued to cloud windows.
Cigarette smoke floated about the ceiling.
Moments lingered like hours.
Disheveled women came inside
and went out laughing too loud
about money, good times and
having offered themselves
for drinks.

The fat white man laughed even louder
self inflicted by his joyless tales
of ships, other countries
and dejection unresolved
in glasses of beer.

Then the swinging door revealed
red, yellow, blue and
green umbrellas moving
briskly pass, sometimes
folding to be rested inside.
Windows began clearing and
I sat comforting an uneasiness,
no more bubbles caressed my glass;
emptiness stood in stillness
the stone faced men had gone
the loud women
had also gone and
the fat white man paid his bill
forcing the bartender's eyes
to move without seeing me.
Neither of them knew my name
or bothered to ask.

I placed my money in front of me.
The bartender gave me back change
without saying a word.

And without tipping I arose
without leaving a word about
who I was or
where I had been or
what ship had held my stories.

Then dazzling rain touched my face,
holding gently like the touch
of a mother's arms. I tasted
the cleanliness of nature, sensing
the stroking touch of its arm-held wind
moving without causing a sway
or fear-thoughts of darkness
for the color of my face was held;
the arms of contentment
cheered my name, folding
me to safety.

CONVERSATION AT A BAR

In a bar we sit and react
I, a total success, least
that's what I tell myself and with
you, I can not connect from
where you're coming from; but
we sit and react anyway, spending
hours drinking beer, meditating,
confusingly cursing each other in
rhythm, hoping tomorrow, when
we meet at 8:45 a.m. to punch the clock
you'll not mention anything
about this conversation.

A SOLDIER'S RETURN

Like trees, staggering
in overspent wind, a soldier
waits for processing
relieved, knowing
"WAR IS OVER"
without victory in View Nam;
feeling arm stretched relief in
newspapers world wide,
relieving his hunched
tired back, longing for gleam
in the warmth of familiar
ground, home where sun
melts in the cool of night.

He has smelled death,
snail laid clouds have hung
like winter's long stems of
burnt grass dipped into icy graves;
but he holds onto remembered tales
of home, even change
he's hoping to be
among new heroes...

News leak...
(no one at home is cheering,
a president forgets,
mentions only how a whole
country can not change
the will of God)
greed gains
mothers lose.

All the soldiers leave
a megillah laying undisturbed,
having watched children die
diversions un-sustained
pieces of earth moved from
one grave to another, he's
watched faces meeting each other
inside of two-sided mirrors
leaving tear stains on both.

He is an unchained prisoner
unthinking now, how times
change, how soon shades of winter
flicker, still matching clothes
but old woes merely sit waiting,
holding on to yesterday's cries
injustice, reawakening pain
so an old war breathes again.

Thinking heroes have long been saluted
in World War I, World War II,
parading flags flew, drums beat...
they lay, even now, face up in books;
The dove will return.
The streets will dance.
Old men will beam in
red, white and blue.

But he will know for sure soon
when TV cameras subside
war protesters lie down
pedantic speeches are said,
airport quietness blossoms;
he will see the unfinished work
weaver birds, still fighting
for rights, protesting wrong

tasks unchanged by time.

SEPTEMBER WIND AND A FRIEND
(to my father)

Viewing his harvested fields
he contemplates the beginning
of fall time leaves and winter.
He whispers to his friend, the wind,
what secrets time has taught
while revealing nothing to the leaves.
His back aches where labor
has wrought less in splendor;
but branded ownership, yet
his prayers have been fulfilled and
he has weathered the storms again.
And touching him with my eyes
is like a sieve in the air,
for he neither nods nor refuses
but sits on an old fallen tree
watching patches of clouds move
at the commands of a friend.

CHANGES
(for Moses Adams)

And Lord how things have changed here
I race now through these pastures
into wide opened plains, plunging through
opened woods and dried fields that father
once cultivated. Where did all his sweat go?
What did he earn? Just a pocket full of
someone else's dirt, sharecropped tears
that I finally understood yesterday
while I walked, looking for traces
hoping to feel one damp spot;
and so today I explode
I creep upon all these trees and bushes
and do the will of my mind
without thoughts of yesterday
when it was understood that I
should be contented.

A SMALL CIRCLE
(of friends)

A bar
A meaningful song
A drink of gin
A napkin
A stool to sit on
A bystander to agree
    Or disagree with
A sadness
A hope
A chance
A thought
about myself, my disadvantages
and the place I would be a king,
                  home.

INDIFFERENCE II

Mine
is
a swan
grace
majestic
like a dance
that must be danced
life
totality
indifference
or
has it come
the time
to define words
anew?

THE CAKEWALK

Three steps forward
two steps backward
all turn around
Black folks with
      rhythmic strides
walking to a beat
told to stop
look down
      then
docile-like
they wonder why
their numbers aren't called
never realizing
or understanding
      games
the ins and outs
of political games
      where
winners are chosen
long before
Election Day when
it really doesn't matter
if there's going to be
      a cakewalk.

A PHOTO ALBUM

Spring always rushed to meet us
we greeted its aroma in readiness
summer tiptoed in, at times
without ample warning.
Even though we watched you
paint pictures of uniqueness
in each moment, we forgot to exhale;
harboring regrets, noting how
we had barely gotten use to burning sun
listening to dried wood speak about
roasting hot dogs in back yards
adding mustard and ketchup on bread
sipping ice cold lemonade before
summer would end, a moment
each year, forgotten in euphoria
before fall leaves lay down
         to sleep in winter.

We forgot to keep in mind how
nothing is forever that lives
we may spend a lifetime trying
to recapture smiles, the redness of roses
the airy touch of a baby's hand or
its first tooth shown without shame
landscapes of rain showers drenching
across the way, leaving laughter
to caress life reached upward;
but now, sadness, we may not be able
        to retain memory.

Then we searched, opening secrets
folded like persimmon beer and fall fruit
preserve, exposing portraits you had
so carefully hidden all the time
in the center of those
        big brown eyes.

CHOOSING

With limitless places to go,
chances to slip into choice life
we huddle in this uninspiring tenement
immured in a has-been room where
cast-iron air lay and Hobson's choice
evokes little anger.

We exist in the painful air puffs
floating with its distant dreams
thriving solely on yesterdays excuses
when we both could still function
without innovation, self resolve
or well-thought-about choices;

Even now, unable to imagine the missing
lock on this cage door, how we could
simply lift ourselves up and by
placing one foot in front of the other
walk, we know, we will not, for
we both worship these walls

Without hearts, echoing the mixed
discussions about an outside world
a resolve, a formula, a kite string…
each time, having almost
understood simple instructions
we will choose not to be
                    powerful once more.

CHOICES

In silence I can only pray for you
my barrel of salient options
drained, no remaining choices
unopened, only dashed hopes
flames that lift like raving blares.
I, having held my own hands
outstretched, to impart choices
between mistakes and success,
vent now, my raging frustration
grappling in air as I watch
your perpetual opposition
to the obvious need for change
from a putrefied existence.

Even in my silence, I still live
within you and wait to glimpse
again the brightness of your eyes
when they would lift like those
of a five day old baby whose
visions are focused for the first time.

DOING FINE

You watch him but he doesn't mind.
You advise him but he doesn't listen.
Soon you ignore him but with understanding for
He has chosen without thought, to pretend
That he's doing fine, unassisted.

You hear of him in time and sigh.
You still wish for him life's happiness
But chances have not changed, things are
The same as they were when you knew him then.
Only now, doing fine
Is in his mind
Bolted down.

TWO LINES CONNECTING

I watched the SISTER
riding on the "A" train
accepting contributions
            for the Lord
The BROTHER
from the MOVEMENT
passed her THEIR position paper
asked her to take heed.
She took it, extending
her graceful smile, saying
"We are all God's children" and
offered him a small bible
            in exchange
                        but
the brother waved her off
shaking his head
mumbling FOOL
            not interested.

But what did I expect?
The brother never did pass
Communications 101
            even after
                        taking it
                                    THREE times!

DELUSIONS

When we dream so hard
wish for so much and
fool ourselves for so long
our lives become one example
of a disarrayed nightmare
unable to see the miracle
when it happens.

Revish Windham

**Pain oozed
out as darkness
enfolding daylight**

Revish Windham

HER CROWN OF THORNS

I held my camera ready
focusing on her frightening/
pleading eyes as they gleamed
pointing deep, exposing
petrified-held moments of
its perplexed owner, no longer able
to control pain, overwhelmed by
frequent and deranged laughter

I noted the coulisse of
makeshift etchings on
uncounted card boards
surrounding her shopping cart.
The mystery was deepened and did not
explain why she had concluded
the world "is crazy" or that the
people "lack compassion" and
she's "waiting for change."
Why, I ask, would she wait?

In my attempt at understanding
my mind focused on the thesaurus
of her body, grasping for reasons
explaining the difference between
her portraying the condition
suggestive of disgrace and
the proclamation of a star
experiencing moments of jubilation
yet displaying mismatched eyes
momentarily registering
a standing ovation.

I centered on her lack of design
messages deep-dyed over
card boards:

> "bringing awareness
> lost fame reappearing
> reoccurring applauds
> bringing down a house, provoking
> repeated curtain calls
> a final accolade
> on Broadway"

Still I walked behind her
photographing a treasury of years
preserving a has-been richness
a frame that is now folded, hips
overworked, overwrought
ebony hands hanging from a
white crayon-plastered face
turning its mouth to speak
of a reason alien to
what the camera sees

Others were also shopping
going in and out of stores.
They too watched her, most
reacting in their own discernment
stretching their necks to keep memory
of a displayed weather beaten
eighteenth century theater stage

> used by a cast of one
> who is unrecognized...
> trying to identify the star
> take their own photograph
> explain what is missing
> from yesterday.

But unlike them, I had
almost from the beginning
understood her pains, touched
her sky, recognized why it made sense
that the ocean had become filled
with her tears. And too, I was tolerant
of my own need to save her and
the time I spent seeking to dilute
her exuding compassion, move it
back to a controlled state.

I watched her shattered cone shape
at times bend down, the veins rising
atop her hands, like blossoms
protecting "imagined gold" cradled
in opulent shopping carts, held
onto with Samson-like strength

Finally
with no more film
my need to save her
surrendered
she passed me
and I, unable
to alter the condition
could only stare and note how
elegantly she wore her crown
how she had finally etched
a perfect illusion of a street
forcing it to turn
down an alley and
disappear into stale air
the card boards still flickering
causing a neon breeze
like a glow folding/unfolding
exclaiming used/dispossessed/baffled

screaming/proclaiming
without a tether but frozen
an irretrievable woman
arrayed in overcoat grace
a crown of thorns displayed
a moonstricken soloist rising
to perform her next aria.

A BEAUTIFUL FEELING
(for Rita's unborn child)

If piercing your oceans' heart
lifts you upward, providing
tiny raindrops in resolve,
I am sure you would discover
a uniqueness, a quiet sensation
like you have never known,
a feeling of power latched on,
a dare to control arisen, a part of
an exuberant world in which
you live would then radiate;
you would finally know joy
feel comfort for childhood tears
harmonized in those brackish
inhered pathetic years, gain
a new outlook, allowing a new life
to swell, opening the way for it
to breathe and you to ooze out
no longer fettered, finally
an ocean in control of
how your tides flow
allowing that which dwells
therein to ripple in peace.

BIRD WOMAN

I watch her communicate with birds
　in the park, on streets or
　wherever birds converge.

I watch her gently spread crumbs
　stale bread or saltine crackers
　so carefully she does it, all the time
　sitting down or standing in her old age
　shoes, draped in a weather worn cloak
　a seasoned hat adorning her head.

I watch the birds and listen to their aside whispers,
　enjoying their dance, observing how they
　light expertly to the ground, pecking
　fighting for an occasional spot
　on her shoulders, without thoughts of her
　as human, rather a source of kindness
　a mound of earth bringing worms
　for breakfast in early morning.

They trust her, a bundle of love and
I believe she understands. For them,
　she is the one who covered them as eggs
　catered to their opened beaks and now
　returned as the bird woman.

TO BE LINDA AGAIN

Now a desolate woman
wrapped, without intention, in a new
unimportant name, embedded in
a stigma of homelessness,
amnestic of how it was once
when she was Linda and first
dreamed of northern cities, when
home in the arms of family or
sleeping in a child's warmth on
chicken and geese feathered mattresses,
getting up at night only to pee,
stomach full, having had fun
all day, not even a dream
that hell would be born.

II

Her life, entrenched in hopelessness,
is without intestinal fortitude,
her suppurated innards are wrapped
without alteratation, an unvisited forest of
shame; the store she slumbers in front of
is opening soon, she will move,
no longer able to hide outside in
night-time idleness.

III

She's a disreputed woman,
having survived another night
where no one sought to take her life or
highlight her make-believe values
nor record irrelevant discoveries;

she will keep only colors, for her deep
well of laughter will go still unheard
and she'll not recapture the subject
of dreams of Linda as a child.

IV

She would like to revisit
that which use to be; but she's been
a part of too much disfavor,
having too many dreams deferred,
she's done too much, in shame, surviving,
whoring, stealing, losing her soul,
times welcoming dying.
There are no more smiles
to cherish or remember,
too much hurt when
forcing the face to beam;
anyway, to be Linda again
would take more time
than there is for her to live.

HEART BEAT

Hearts live.
They cannot die
but continue to flow after
the candles go out.
They always try teaching
how it is worthwhile,
at least once, to allow
its pith to experience
touching of another's beating
its rhythmic sashay
wrapping wind in
the same swing
a body dancing
to the same music
following the same flow
as the other.

FOR A GHETTO CHILD
(and with thoughts of Johnny Samuels)

Hurry, Michael,
start climbing the success ladder.
Don't you dare lose
                    the fight.

Be as unyielding as the rock, vowing
you will not be moved.
You will
            withstand the worst
                        of storms.

Then,
            One step at a time.
                        Go on, step.
You will make it
            for when you
                        feel the vibes
                        you'll see
                                    the way.

Hurry, Michael.
Hurry now, child.
The wind will lift you.
                    Now step!

WHERE THERE IS NO RAINBOW

With a million and one places
to go, they slip into fitted costumes
fashioned by designers of failure.

They huddle in small chilled places
draped in penury, touching shadows
enveloped in once fun-filled space
where the darkness never leaves and
cast iron feathers are laid.

They pray for different actualities
without thoughts of creating the rainbow.
Fixated restraints hold them
without resistance, in their emptiness
they're thriving on pains of yesteryears
holding on to the forgotten thin rail-bars,

Practicing dance before cloaking mirrors
glued to never-again-sky-filled memories
unable to lift shades, peek out and
realize the images inside are frozen
preventing their collapsing minds
from using the chance to be free.

They hold the failures
ever so tightly in place
ignoring the colors of a rainbow.

Like caged birds, they wait only
for the door to be opened.

A LETTER FROM ROBERTO

Dear Mom,

I didn't believe in shedding tears
when hurt, nor did I understand then
why, for in my haste to experience
solutions, I melted into el barrio
dressing in its image of
toughness, I came to dislike altogether
that which you believed and
I now see as the answer to
a child's promise
directions.

God!

I could never speak before
of how I stabbed life
a thousand times in
an adopted mind
racing to be driven
by a never quieting fire.

So, today
an inmate for life
my first letter comes
in unearthed chips, hoping
you understand why
so much of me flew away
when my feathers first developed into
a macho self-made image
and it danced and I
soared into its
dreams clouded gray.

Too late
we both now grieve for
lack of answers, watching
pictures never ever before seen
which is why we both grab the air,
smiling at loose wind.

I do hope you understand and
feel all the love I've folded herein
held together by a memory of when
you last cried.

Roberto

JUSTICE

The people dance up elevators
holding tears, down and up, knowing.
Mothers hurting, lawyers casing winner's
lists, judges rejecting change morning into
evening, all sitting, mothers questioning
nothing, fathers serving life or less
children crying sometimes over two lines
revolving through flying doors, looking
without seeing or understanding
no walking or smoking signs
kangaroo court in session...
the record stops, they lose
without decoding messages
or resolving a baffle. A panacea
of nothing is made into
wall flowers, unmoved;
they rise, bumping their heels
against solid benches
that never move.

THE SUMMER WE REMEMBERED
(summer before last)

The photos manifest
themselves before us
country landscapes, early evenings
grass-worn front yards
children frolicking
posing unrestricted
feet undaunted, exploring plots
of sun-baked sand, ignoring
the soles itching from
day before sand-spur pain

Children, whose eyes
reflectively divert, interlock
briefly, amazed at sand lizards
racing across imaginary desserts
momentarily believing
they've solved why
animals vanish and
re-incarnate themselves
another day

In stillness!

It was impossible
freedom forever danced
     under a limitless sky
smiles/laughter came quicker
than boyish-lungs could breathe.

Minds continuously exaggerating
painting multi-characters in
a rustic picture of
    a once in a lifetime sun set
    cricket choirs chanting
    bull frog lullabies rendered
    questioning night owls
remaining hidden out of sight...
    and finally without fanfare
    everything, even the trees wailed
    about seeing dusk creep in
    outside that small town
        in Alabama.

Now, looking at you
    all grown up
I'm still amazed, digesting
how we are still sworn to secrets
kept since before the last summer
when we posed
    unrestricted.

A GIFT TO MY BROTHER
(August 1976)

We will always remember the good years
that are now considered past.
We will understand the uniqueness
living in each of us to this moment.
We will, in your absence, continue
to speak of that which we had and
accept the reality that yours, like
all of life, had to someday cease,
return to God who gives it and
takes it away, when a life is swept
away as seeds to someday grow
again, be smiling blossoms
and a facsimile of Him who
governs the entire universe.

ON BROKEN WINGS

On broken wings she sails into
an unknown horizon, understanding
little of all the danger—those who
would deflate her stride and take little
winds and toss them against the main road.

She has no bother of time for
she believes there has always been
and will always be time to do things
presented in the preamble.

Her dress is puffed like empty breasts.
She swings higher than before, even further
and her nights never require the sun
to settle down in hiding, nor wait
for a new day or morning.

On broken wings she still counts stars
in open display, the same as, long ago,
explaining why we never connected…

How we could have been a single soul
flowing between two bodies instead of
one soaring alone on broken wings.

PREPARING FOR THE STORM
(for Vicky, I hope you made it)

I've watched my little girl grow up
innocent, the epitome of it,
smiling unto the world, believing
all people are truly her friends,

Believing that no one would ever hurt
or harm the slightest hair, but I
try warning her that there are also those
who would call her other

Than her name, those who would
hit her for little reasons, and
those who would take her life if
she is not careful to be alert.

I teach her that even if she
grows into a mighty oak tree, strong,
there is still the danger of a hurricane;
without protection, even it will break

Against the stronger winds. Oak trees
seldom bend, they just crack
when pushed too far, too long.
God, I hope she understands.

Revish Windham

**Perpetuated love
insures the taste
of a first breath
every morning**

Revish Windham

OUR GREATEST DANCE

Though we danced times before,
our wedding dance will never fade.
That day we discovered a different rhythm
a different exuberance projecting beyond
all prior understanding. The song, "You Are
So Beautiful To Me," opened God's arms
and we sate cupid's arrow. You perfected
a ballerina's grace and I, intoxicated
from the euphoria, floated
on the wings of its wind.

It was an unworn scenario, melting in
master music, us whirling, watching
accepting smiles, watching faces glow,
those who came to transmit happiness
to hold hands with us from across
the room, raising their glasses in
salute, ignoring the existence of
limited time, praying non-verbally
for us to be crowned, earning
blue ribbons, our hearts always united
beating as one conquered mountain
reaching into its once
unexplored clouds.

Yes, we danced times before
but merged, one step, bound
without double prints or distressing
a world-held arm-aura, ceding only
to God's entourage, His glancing
perfection, you and I were floating with
His blessings, given His most
precious gift, to care for each other
until death do we part. This fusion
was indeed our greatest dance.

THE WIND WHISPERS

Black woman, listen;
you are my woman and I
an ever present wind
holding weightlessly as
like immaculate whispers
     flowing
      everywhere.

I have sought.
I have grown.
Catch me cause
I need you to
hold fast and
   believe
    in my dream.

I love you
   Black woman.

A MOMENT
(for Janice)

Today I felt gold bricks
beneath my feet
like a bookend
I stood without falling over
I felt tiny bubbles tingling
against my soul
like taking a shower using love gel
Today I lived
Today I became
Today I was one
with you

COMFORT

Last night
I marveled
Savoring moments merged
Reaching a climax, experiencing
The core of breathlessness

We, recognized eased answers
Flowing together in endlessness
Sampling the feel of
Silver rivers dancing, playfully down
Golden carved mountains

And finally listening to your silence
Softness so like a lamb's breath
The quietness of late moon rising
I felt the blissfulness of
Naked tranquillity.

SUNDAY MORNING IS

God's gift, an unscheduled awakening
sometimes escorted by rain clouds
or hushed night-held snow
undisturbed, mounted as
an artist's creation, a painting
of God explaining what
one-day beauty is, His
genesis, a rare chance to
take a day off to rest,
move into a different agenda,
including mid-day absurdities
more lovemaking, caressing
tender thighs still warm
from last night's under-quilt
dancing; Sunday morning is
when you think "up" and
pray, thankful each time,
however it comes.

THE ENCHANTMENT
(of the soul sister's' dance)

I felt the vibrations, even before the
words began, you moving your body
with the grace of a gyrating swan.

I watched you lift your head
eyes closed, fingers popping, face beaming
like sunlight, you breathing rhythm with
the taste of sweet-wild-plums
emitted among wind-floating-flower
petals and dried leaves.

I watched the sweat roll slowly
then swiftly like rivers down
your African mountainsides.

I watched your firm breast rise
and speak, your entire body moving,
in rocking motions, your
hips swaying, never missing
a beat...I watched you melt
in the sun, succumbing to
Marvin Gay's "Sexual Healing."

RIDING UP EIGHTH AVENUE TO HARLEM

I took a bus home from work today,
waited a long time for one to come,
at least 45 minutes, four finally came,
                              in a row,
three were crowded, so I took the fourth
it too looked crowded, until I realized
everybody was standing up front, didn't
                    necessarily have to be.
Made my way pass big butts
overstuffed pocketbooks,
umbrellas, used shopping bags, folded
baby carriages, shopping carts...phew!
                    Another day's work.

Would you believe
      there were some seven empty seats
                              in the back.
Sat myself down.
Took out my newspaper
so I could catch up on the news...
And just as I was about to get into
What's happening in Kosovo
      I hear this duet
      across from me,
      doing a number...chewing gum
      just popping and popping!
Laughing and conversing
about two other women, as if they were
the only ones on the bus who had witnessed
            something and everybody else
just loves to hear gum popping and them
talking about how yesterday
            Tamika beat the shit out of Milika.

My man, next to me, held on to his brown paper bag
and every now and then he'd take a swig,
    smelled just like he'd worked all day
                    in the brewery.

In the corner, Big Trae played his radio
so loud, it felt just like I was
in the middle of a disco.

Then would you believe at every stop
everybody who was getting off
just had to pull the bell string...
can you imagine all the dings?
          Ding, ding, ding, ding!
                Geeeeze!

Then this little brat, sitting next to me
          decided he wanted
to get a better view from the window
by standing upon the seat, shoes dirty
and all over me. His mother, I guess that was
who she was, never stopped reading
               "the Star."

Then Bilbo, the Gorilla, got on.
Boy, did he look mean, like
if you'd look at him the wrong way
he'd bite your head off.
        Only thing, he hadn't taken a bath
and what could I do?
I wasn't going to tell him
he could use some soap and water.

After a while somebody cursed out the driver
calling him a f...ing bastard.
Some guy called another, wearing glasses
a four-eyed mother f...er
accusing him of making passes at his girlfriend
who seemed to have enjoyed the whole thing.

Two teenagers opened windows
to yell out to some buddies, then
forgot to close them,
letting all the cold air come in...

Then, I just couldn't believe my nose
when Crazy Eddie got on.
He had to have eaten "garlic a la garlic"
for lunch. Phew!
Was it a relief when he got off after three stops.
The smell stayed on for three more.

Across the way, on the floor
I caught a glimpse of
two roaches making rounds,
and a beer bottle that had been left
was rolling from one side of the bus
to the other.

Finally the bus gets to 125th Street.
I pulled the string to ring the bell
but the thing didn't work and before I
could get the driver's attention
he'd sped past my stop.
I said to him
"your bell thing didn't ding."
He just shrugged his shoulder
saying "sorry pal."

So I got off at the next stop
walked back one block and over,
headed for the Club Baby Grand, a few doors
from the Apollo Theater to get
myself a stiff one.

I said, hey bartender!
Wanna hear about my day?

Revish Windham

Spirituality
change
blues
leaving footsteps
forgiven
times in sadness
joy
when
Black folks travel

Revish Windham

DUSTY BLUES

I'm waiting, trying to understand why
things just get harder when thinking
without solutions, praying without
sun to gleam from, hoping another
drink will submerge me into that which
causes dust to rise into the blue of heaven,

Feeling you look at me, remembering
your sashay, sensing your spicy breath
even from across that room, you touching
without reaching your hand out or even
searching into my eyes to see if I hurt;
you, not giving a damn about anything.

The music wrangling about two bodies making
love, four arms unrestrained like meshed wire
curved about itself; you, even from way over
there, displaying questions about the day before
when I believed in all that I held, listening
to you say it would be gigantic, a stone, unmoved.

So today I write blues, dusty blues, while
looking at others but seeing your image, being
reminded about your eyes, lips, us making love
finding the spirit of Nivana, euphoric moments
exploding; I sit gnawed, holding a glass of gin
watching the ripples go out and roll back in.

TABULA RASA

Have you changed?
I wonder, had you known me
yesterday, would you have touched and
felt the same, your paint brush stroked
with neutral passion as I then preached
about making hell and heaven choices?

Would the colors mixed have lifted a soft sky
blue, from then a white owned river where
I spoke about the devil digging upward
when I lived next door to Mississippi?
Did you have cold gray jaundiced eyes?

Today you painted a portrait of a strong
brave and passionate Black man, me
orating out of Africa's past, lifting a
veil from a rainbow-awed gathering
at the edge of soft pale blue water.
Have you really changed?

WHOSE BLUES

Folded in his seated position, he clutches
a lusterless horn, using his ebbing breath
and bubble gum cheeks to explain, he holds
his own moments, creating blossoms, his
music flows like a well-rested morning.

Then, with his eyes closed (only he knows
the real color his eyes change into),
the blossoms transfigure even more, blues notes
lifting into the bare innards of his spirit,
and finally, it is no longer important
that I do not see his eyes, for I too
am folded, seated, if only for the moment,
in the same seat as he sits in, breathing
the same air, unaware the color of my eyes
has also changed, I am touching the blossoms,
my own soul is succumbing, humming, breathing
blues, experiencing heaven.

Then, I watch you too, gazing,
inquiring about my unseen eyes,
wondering as I did, whose blues?

MARCHING FOR HOPE

They said my
song was sad,
made them cry
search for understanding.
They said they eventually
could also feel the pain
throbbing profusely from
my magnanimous heart
recognize aged scars
they had helped
to fixate there.

Which explains why,
now (unlike before
when fear painted mere
pictures of hopelessness
showing people breathing
but unable to feel air
as it passed through
their hearts)
we're sitting,
harmonizing like a choir
experiencing a new beginning,
examining the civil war
we've ended.

FLOWING LIKE A RIVER
(Junior, James, Charles and I)

We were created brothers
our blood will forever
flow united in spirit, our
joys will exude from memory as
will our tears bleed from hurt,
like the ocean, we are
replete, deep and without
shallow water; even though
we appear, at times, painted in
a tone of depth-less-ness,
we will forever know that
every time heaven clears
its throat our river-veins
will be at ready to rise and sing
with steel-like voices and
stand undivided, unchallenged,
because, unlike parade streamers
our plasma dances without
limits, restraints or fears
as we each hold onto the
others oversized hands
leaf-floating,
brothers following
the flow of a river
from where it began
to where it never ends.

THE ASHES BURN FOREVER
(Friday, May 5, 1995)

Still he lives.
Like everlasting embers
forever leaping into flames
his dregs breathe within us.

Brown colored prints of him:
a hero, a dreamer, a pioneer,
are all safely tucked
in a side closet, between
pages of an over-used dust-covered book
protected between new editions
current issues in a file drawer
among handwritten letters describing
first-time steps taken to focus on
a people's progress and history.

And yes, like you I too reserve treasures
memories of forty, thirty-five
twenty-five years ago when Leroy Jones
shook his hand, Sammy Davis Jr.,
Maya Angelo, Langston Hughes
Chester Hines, J. A. Rogers,
James Baldwin and so many
more were photographed beside him
always smiling into a projected glean
from him into a dream-turned reality.

Too soon his body surrendered
his face displaying its fifty years
and ten years beyond, crows feet
dancing a spider's web-tango, labor
was etching outward, his frame

pressing inside, his back
memorializing the arch of
a rainbow beginning to sink into
tired hips, into rare gold found
but hidden and without having
been fully evaluated...
Explaining why we were
all saddened, watching
his arched back, his face
holding fish-closed eyes
center-protruding wrinkles, his
slur-breaking voice trying
to explain where he had been
where he had planned to go
but could not because there
was no more road.

Thus it is explained why
he erected a museum
and you and the others stand now
eyes gaped, looking at me
leafing through
yesterdays' file drawers
reaching into forty, thirty-five
thirty and twenty-some years
of his achievements, helping you
in your understanding, even
without knowing all, yet clearly seeing
not a broken spirit, but a hero's soul
photographed, and you looking
watching his rainbow's end
gold frames, exuding memories
that will always be his embers
occasionally leaping
into flame.

WALKING
(keeping history alive)

You go walking
down
the same streets
hearing
the same voices
feeling
the cold breezes
counting aged footsteps
one
two
three.

Each time is a beginning
a start of time when
night forces laughter to hush
stop along the way
without slumber
in memory
dreaming
listening to the sounds
more than three hundred years
depth, not a child's
moans in filth, tears, death
the riffle of water
soothing terror to sleep, but

remembering Africa
from the beginning
insomniac players
of music, drums beating life
breathing even in enmity.

Resting?
Mindless fastidious
gigantic images of night
sleeping with eyes wide open
memory encoding
unrehearsed screams
about dancing
then walking…
counting footsteps
measuring each wave
flinging out into unseen night
yet arms keeping time
with feet
one
two
three
leaving prints
each time.

SPENDING TIME

They hold onto bent backs,
used eyes barely peeking out
wrought hands and tired limbs,
all symbolic of old men seeking
companionship, recalling lost wives,
misguided youth, unlucky unions, friends.

They sit on dirty benches
united in a park or just strolling
with eternity, listening to yesterday's
happiness or fading pain.

Then there is that moment of silence.
It is time to go home and wait
with hope tomorrow comes.

THE FORGIVEN

There you sit, listening
to the people remember
his pushed out cheeks, his
unrehearsed jokes about life;
the people, now dancing with glee
but you're sitting, drowning in remorse
for that which was done by you
praying you'll not remember
in time the pains you carry.

You, wailing ever so quietly;
but the people are not listening
even as you whimper in faintness
trying to offer reasons, show
a bounced out heart, explain
why you should be forgiven,
remembered for past pulsation,
and not for once upon a time
when a harebrain jumped
without restraints
taking a pound of life
from someone else.

Perhaps you will someday forget.
Perhaps you will again hear
the pummel, once peace
of a arm-held quietness
when you lay down
all forgiven.

THE JOURNEY

Many years ago my thoughts floated
like dried leaves on a windy day.
My mind, upward-laid open, taking in all
that glowed, all that the wind lifted.
But there were the times it held firm
grasping my father's preciseness
my mother's refinement, without
thoughts then of one day, maybe
fifty years in the future, I'd be
sitting with my own son sharing
these circumstances of history.

Mornings I'd wake to the penetrating
aroma of country-cured ham, bacon,
listening, as I arose, to teakettle whistles,
my mother, Lillie's soft voice, humming
reminding us that it was time, chores to be
done, God had granted us another day

I remember mirroring my father, laying
like a shadow behind his bent forward back
as he plowed in a field of growing cotton,
while rows of Ireland-green corn smiled,
smelling the wind blown squalidness of
stable mules, responding only to harness
and their rein's suggestions, guided by the
gee and haw directions of my father's hands.

Times my thoughts traveled into books
pictures, stories I'd read or children's games.
Never once retaining the thought of farmers
deserving dishonor or shame for I knew
eventually, for me there would be

no more fields of cotton or growing corn
in my assembled life, yet times would come
when I'd cherish the memory, sense the
touch of downy softness, the smell
of corn yellowing and miss hearing
morning awakened country roosters
lifting their heads, routine calls
for the sun to rise into the center
of the sky, then float downward
until it's hidden by the night.

I remember watching the lifting veins
on my mother's over-worked hands,
the too many wrinkles surrounding
her eyes, savoring her voice, tired but
strong enough to shake wind as it touched.
Then reaching for my father's used hand
holding onto like vice-grips, the roughness
of his contact never justifying a hurt mark
always exuding assurance and promise.
I remember the rushing flow of African
strength gushing from their hands through
mine into an unfolding soul.

Many years later, having taken the journey from
there to here, enjoying occasional revisits,
having gone from coloured to Black, I sit now
among bright orange day lilies, in between
mounds of sage bushes, using the same
hands without wrinkles, no over-used
voice, the same soul, same strengths...
and if you listen, you'll hear the drum
beats, rhythmic sounds of bare-feet,
sounds of Middle-Passage-breathing,
arms moving oars, back and forth
to a drum beat, boom, boom, boom...

Revish Windham

**I've come
to understand
the journey**

IN MY BLACKNESS
(with thanks to my Mother & Father)

I am that I am. Cool.
I make no excuses for me.
I am all Black. I invent.
I teach. I create. I lead. I follow.
I sometimes win and sometimes I lose.
And yes, I love music, I sing opera,
        country, blues, pop and I rap too.

I've been the creator of many
wonders, even those you didn't
at first accept, legitimize or
give me the credit for; those
that were stolen and eventually
        called your own.

My blackness flows throughout
my body, in every ounce of my blood, flowing
through my veins as a precious breath of air.
It hugs and squeezes, creating an
endless staircase, one like you could
never climb or guess the height because
despite your sounding like me, dressing
like me and wanting to be like me,
you can never be as Black as I am,
and that's okay too, because I can never
be as who-ever-it-is-you-are
        as you are.

I have my memories. I've had pains.
joys and I have unresolved moments in my mind.
For in my blackness, I too chance, I learn
and I have tried things:
to be inclusive, to integrate, pitching
curved baseballs in your direction but
you were not always a player, only a fan
       and couldn't catch store brand baseballs.

We even pretended a few times to be friends,
you came to my home and drank beer
in my living room while we both laughed at
       Jimmy Walker saying "Dyn-o-mite!"

You know, you never did say exactly
what it was you liked about me,
whether it was my superfly hat,
my Coltrane music, or the poetry books I was
reading by Nikki Giovanni and Langston Hughes,
or maybe it was as you said one time,
in jest, how you thought I
needed to be made over.

But it doesn't matter, now.
I've concluded my own study and accept
me as I am and don't need anyone else's
acceptance to be. I don't
have to get caught up in anyone
else's confusion; you don't have to
travel with me to D.C. for I already
       have 999,999 going there with me.

It's okay that you're still wearing
peace signs around your neck and talking
about free love, it's just that it's not my
stick and I don't need it to lean on

I can manage on my own, for
I am an established institution
dedicated to hope, decorated
in the pride of knowing
        I am somebody.

My blackness has moved me through
slavery, the underground, the emancipation,
lunch counter sit-ins, pimp-mobiles, hippie
wakes and poetry reading about Black power;
it's taken me places I'd only dreamed
existed. So you're damn right, I am elated!

I still got my bellbottom pants and
platform shoes and I have pictures of me in them
all tucked away in my Black pride closet,
including thoughts of me strutting down
a Soul Train line on Saturday morning.
It'll all be there recorded
        in my history.

Yes, in my blackness I am not always
angry; many times I am gentle.
I am kind and I treat other people
with mutual respect. I don't ask for special
consideration, just what it is I give,
give it back to me. I can take it
        anyway it comes, whatever the shape.

You see, I am already. I am. And
unlike the Native American, I do not
need to be singled out, discovered
or made to be civilized.
        I really am.

In my blackness, I am also blind.
I refuse to see what you see, especially
if it's a different me you are trying
                to get me to be.

So, you see, I'm doing alright
in my blackness. Like a butterfly
I am free. I think I
might even find the end
of a endless staircase.
In my blackness, you know
I can almost do anything I
        set my mind to
                in my blackness.
                                Yeah!
Yeah!

Revish Windham

ACKNOWLEDGEMENTS

Going Nowhere Fast first appeared in Living Lyrics anthology, "Best Contemporary Poetry," 1967.

Changes, Do You Know My Name, Saturday Night (all with some variations) and Indifference first appeared in Shades of Black, 1970.

A Small Circle first appeared in Shades Of Anger, 1972.
Conversation At The Bar first appeared in Ashes To Ashes, 1974.

September Wind And A Friend first appeared in Black Forum Magazine, 1975.

To Be Linda Again first appeared (with slight variations) in Black Forum Magazine, in the winter 1976-77 issue.

Preparing For The Storm first appeared in "American Poetry Anthology," Vol. IV, No. 1, 1985.

It's Cry Clown, Cry first appeared in Poetry Press Anthology, "Reflections," 1989.

Doing Fine appeared in the National Library of Poetry, "Days of Future's Past, 1989.

On Broken Wings first appeared in Sparrowgrass Poetry Forum, Treasured Poems of 1989.

Whose Blues first appeared in Sparrowgrass Poetry Forum, Ten Years of Excellence (1988-1998), 1998.

Spending Time first appeared (with slight variation, under the title "Time") in The International Library of Poetry anthology "Secret Hiding Places," 2000.

Mothers first appeared in the Famous Poets Society's anthology, 2000.

About the Author

Revish Windham was born in Panola, Alabama where he graduated from North Sumter High School. He attended Paine College, Augusta, Georgia, and received his Bachelor's degree from Morris Brown College, Atlanta. Later he received his Master's degree in Public Administration form New York University. During his service in the United States Navy, his first poetry was published in "United Poets," and Living Lyrics' anthology "Best Contemporary Poetry 1967." His works have since appeared in many other magazines, anthologies, and newspapers.

Revish began a long career in public service in 1968 beginning with the New York City Department of Social Services as a Caseworker, working with drug addicted individuals. He moved on to the New York State Division for Youth, addressing the needs of delinquent youth and their families. He was certified as a Cultural Awareness and Race Relations Trainer and conducted workshops within the Agency. He later moved on to the New York State Division of Human Rights from which he retired in June of 1999. He was also certified as a New York State Mediator and successfully conducted mediation sessions both within Human Rights and as a volunteer for the New York City Victim Services Agency.

In 1970, Revish was one of five founders of Black Forum, a biannual literary magazine which was published until 1975. Over the years he has received numerous awards, certificates and other forms of recognition for his involvement, achievement and contribution to various worthy causes i.e. listed in *Who's Who in Black America* and *Who's Who in Poets and Writers*.

Revish is a life member of the Morris Brown College Alumni Association, Phi Beta Sigma Fraternity, Inc. and the American Legion – Post 506. He is also a member of the 369th Veterans' Association, Inc. & Auxiliary, Convent Avenue Baptist Church and Prince Hall Free & Accepted Masons and the

Ossining, New York branch of the NAACP. He is a member of the Board of Directors of two not-for-profit community organizations: Southeast Bronx Neighborhood Center, Inc., and Quality Vending Services, Inc.